Everett Baker's
SASKATCHEWAN

PORTRAITS OF AN ERA

Selected by Bill Waiser

FIFTH
HOUSE

Copyright © 2007 Bill Waiser
First published in paperback in 2008

All rights reserved. No part of this publication may be reproduced, stored in a retrieval system, or transmitted, in any form or by any means, electronic, mechanical, recording, or otherwise, without the prior written permission of the publisher, except in the case of a reviewer, who may quote brief passages in a review to print in a magazine or newspaper, or broadcast on radio or television. In the case of photocopying or other reprographic copying, users must obtain a license from Access Copyright.

Cover and interior design by Brian Smith / Articulate Eye
Cover image: 1136. At Climax 4-H Calf Club, May 30, 1956
Map by Brian Smith, funded by The University Publications Fund
All images courtesy Saskatchewan History & Folklore Society, funded by SaskLotteries.
Leica camera illustration by Brian Smith (based on photo by Rama; Creative Commons Attribution ShareAlike 2.0 France licence)
Edited by Kirsten Craven
Proofread by Geri Rowlatt
Scans by Keith Seabrook / ABL Imaging, with digital manipulation by Brian Smith, funded by The University Publications Fund

The type in this book is set in ITC Stone.

The publisher gratefully acknowledges the support of The Canada Council for the Arts and the Department of Canadian Heritage.

We acknowledge the financial support of the Government of Canada through the Book Publishing Industry Development Program (BPIDP) for our publishing activities.

The publisher wishes to thank and acknowledge Saskatchewan History & Folklore Society and its funding agency SaskLotteries for the use of the photographs by Everett Baker printed in this volume.

Hardcover edition:
Printed in Hong Kong
11 10 09 08 07 / 5 4 3 2 1

Paperback
2008 / 01

First published in the United States in 2007 by
Fitzhenry & Whiteside
311 Washington Street
Brighton, Massachusetts, 02135

Library and Archives Canada Cataloguing in Publication Data

Baker, Everett
   Everett Baker's Saskatchewan : portraits of an era / selected by Bill Waiser. -- 1st ed.

Includes bibliographical references and index.
ISBN 978-1-897252-04-8 : ISBN 978-1-897252-45-1 (pb)

   1. Saskatchewan--History--20th century--Pictorial works. 2. Saskatchewan--Biography--Portraits. I. Waiser, W. A. II. Title. III. Title: Saskatchewan.

FC3512.B343 2007   971.24'030222   C2006-906385-0

Fifth House Ltd.
A Fitzhenry & Whiteside Company
1511, 1800-4 St. SW
Calgary, Alberta T2S 2S5

1-800-387-9776
www.fitzhenry.ca

FOR JOURNALIST SCOTT LEITCH

Everett Baker's Saskatchewan

CONTENTS

INTRODUCTION
by Bill Waiser
1

EVERETT BAKER'S SASKATCHEWAN
23

APPENDIX:
THE LEICA CAMERA AND KODACHROME FILM
by Brock Silversides
193

NOTES AND FURTHER READING
197

ACKNOWLEDGEMENTS
199

INDEX
200

ABOUT THE AUTHOR
201

1555. International picnic, Divide, 1953.

INTRODUCTION

ONE HUNDRED DOLLARS WAS A LOT OF MONEY IN 1939. How was he going to justify the purchase—even if it was a good camera? After all, he had just landed a decent job as a field man with the Saskatchewan Wheat Pool, after several hardscrabble years trying to make ends meet on about sixty dollars per month during the Great Depression. It would be a while yet before his money worries were behind him, especially with a family to support. Maybe he was just trying to help out Hugo Haas, the Sudeten refugee who sold him the camera. Then again, the slide photographs he could take could be used to illustrate his presentations as a Wheat Pool field man. Whatever the reasons and despite his personal circumstances, Everett Baker bought the German-made, 35 mm Leica camera. People have been appreciating his photographs ever since.

TO SASKATCHEWAN VIA THE SOO LINE

William Everett Baker was not from Saskatchewan, nor was he a Canadian citizen. But he had a keen understanding of the land's rhythms, its peoples, and its history, and an even keener sense of how to capture this spirit in his photographs. He likely acquired his appreciation of the province and its ways from his years travelling the grid roads, forever meeting people, sharing stories, and talking about the past. His artistic skill with the camera was a matter of talent, an uncanny ability to "see" the scene before him in the lens and press the shutter at the right moment.

Everett was born in January 1893 in Blue Earth county, Minnesota, where his family ran a mixed-farming operation near Janesville. After excelling in high school and earning a scholarship, he attended St. Paul's Hamline University, a Methodist-affiliated institution that reinforced his lifelong aversion to alcohol.

He graduated in 1916 with a bachelor of science degree and would likely have been drafted for war service the following year if not for his asthma. Instead, he took to the road as a door-to-door salesman, peddling *People's Home Library*, a one-volume compendium of practical information on household matters. Despite his soft-spoken nature, Everett had a natural bent for selling, so much so that the book company readily agreed to his request to blaze a new sales territory in southwestern Saskatchewan in the summer of 1917. He hoped the drier climate would be better for his health.[1]

Everett entered Saskatchewan on the so-called "Soo Line," a Canadian Pacific Railway (CPR) branch line that ran northwestward from St. Paul, Minnesota, across the border at Portal through Estevan and Weyburn and on to Moose Jaw. This route had brought tens of thousands of prospective American homesteaders from the Dakotas and Minnesota into Canada in the early twentieth century. Now, it was carrying twenty-four-year-old Baker and his boxes of books.

Everett switched CPR lines at Weyburn and continued west to Kincaid, Saskatchewan, where he began his sales blitz—in his words, "going in blind"—in early April. This time, he set a company sales record—at least fifty orders per week. He made so much money that fall that he bought a half-section farm just outside Aneroid, Saskatchewan (s½, sect. 34, twp 7, range 10, W3rd), about seventy-five kilometres southeast of Swift Current. He planted his first crop the following spring and then travelled to Minnesota to marry his childhood sweetheart Ruth Hellebo, a teacher. The young couple returned to Canada on Dominion Day, 1918.[2]

Baker chose a bad time and a poor location to begin farming. The end of the Great War ushered in a stubborn recession until 1923. The collapse in commodity prices, by as much as seventy-five percent in the case of wheat, doomed small, marginal operations. For the first time in provincial history, the number of farms actually declined in the early 1920s. Many of the abandoned farms were in southwestern Saskatchewan, where there had not been a decent crop since 1916 because of an unrelenting drought. Some had even begun to question whether the region, with its light soils and scanty precipitation, should ever have been put to the plough.[3] Aneroid, named when a CPR crew lost an aneroid barometer near the townsite, was one of those places.

Everett's great farming hopes were humbled by the post-war recession. In seeking to reduce his vulnerability to these kinds of downswings, he became secretary to the Aneroid local of the Saskatchewan Grain Growers' Association in 1919 and actively joined its campaign for some kind of orderly, co-operative marketing. When the federal government refused to establish a national wheat board, he spearheaded the organizational drive in southwestern Saskatchewan to get farmers to sign up for a voluntary, provincial Wheat Pool.[4] He claimed to know many of the people from his bookselling days.

The Baker farm, in the meantime, limped along. A promising potato harvest was lost when the shipment was frozen in the Winnipeg freight yards in 1923. The young couple also had their share of personal tragedy. Their second child, daughter Jean Marie, died before she was one. Everett was also struck down with typhoid fever, followed by a bout with Spanish influenza that nearly killed him. Then his father and two sisters perished in a car crash in Minnesota. Ruth taught school to help keep things afloat, but in 1924 they put the farm up for sale and moved to town. By this point, Everett was convinced that the co-operative movement held the solution to the Saskatchewan farmer's woes and that he could best serve the movement as an organizer, not as a farmer.[5]

THE ANEROID CO-OPERATIVE ASSOCIATION

In 1924, Everett became manager of the Aneroid Co-operative Association. It was the perfect challenge for the former salesman, who also happened to be one of the co-op's founding members. If the new initiative was going to survive and prosper, then who better to run the fledgling business than an ardent believer in the emancipating power of consumer co-operatives? Indeed, Baker had become something of a co-operative evangelist, an irrepressible idealist, and transformed what essentially started out as a simple grocery store into a thriving co-op business selling dry goods, farm machinery, and fuel.[6] He even purchased advertising space on the curtain in the Aneroid theatre.

In 1930, Baker published his thoughts on how Saskatchewan could best move to a truly co-operative society in a small booklet entitled *Working Together: Each for All and All for Each*. "Only as competition gives way to co-operation," he railed against the pitfalls of individualism, "may there be freedom ... from the unequal struggle between the strength of the highly organized and the weakness of the unorganized ... This question of competitive or co-operative methods is the question of the hour."[7]

The success of the Aneroid Co-op had much to do with the long hours Baker unselfishly put into the enterprise. It could also thank the booming wheat economy. Everett's decision to give up farming ironically coincided with the return of better prices and better growing conditions. Farmers responded by growing as much wheat as possible. The 1928 harvest, at almost a third of a billion bushels, was the largest crop ever produced by any province or state in the world up to that time. Settlers in the southwest, meanwhile, seemed to develop amnesia about past drought conditions. Wetter weather encouraged more farmers to take up land in places like Killdeer, Mankota, and Val Marie, or bring more acreage into production. The CPR also overcame its reluctance to build branch lines in the region and laid track in what had up until then been one of the most isolated agricultural districts in Saskatchewan.[8]

Then, the bottom seemed to fall out. At the start of the 1930s, international demand for wheat not only collapsed, but the price went into a free fall. The repercussions were nothing short of catastrophic, all the more so for a province and a people whose livelihood rested almost exclusively on wheat. With expenses outstripping cash receipts, and already carrying a heavy debt load

8613. Everett Baker on horseback, Val Marie, 1957.

from the expansion of the 1920s, many farmers simply could not stay afloat. And when they went down, they took with them other sectors of the provincial economy, like the vortex created by a sinking ship. Few were spared, if only because nearly seven of every ten people, according to the 1931 census, lived and worked in rural Saskatchewan. Many villages and towns, including Aneroid, were pushed to the wall and had trouble providing basic services, let alone meeting their relief responsibilities.

The other nightmare was the prolonged drought that placed a stranglehold on the short-grass prairie district of southern Saskatchewan for most of the decade. Severe droughts had always been a persistent feature, occurring on average every twenty years or so. The 1930s, however, were notorious for the number of consecutive dry years. Hot, drying winds scooped up loose topsoil and whipped it into towering dust storms. Darkness at noon was not uncommon, while churning soil piled up in deep drifts along buildings, fencelines, or ridges. Dirt also seeped into homes, even though people set wet rags on window sills and hung wet sheets over doorways.

Charlotte Whitton, a widely respected social worker and future mayor of Ottawa, was sent by the federal government in the summer of 1932 to examine the distribution of relief in some of the worst hit areas of Saskatchewan. "Driving from Aneroid to Pontiex," she recorded in her handwritten notes in late June 1932, "the country was predominantly desolate ... whole areas were covered with blown soil, ditches filled up, crop barely above ground ... abandoned farms."[9] The situation around Aneroid was no better two years later when a pair of Saskatoon journalists toured the so-called "burnt out" area by car and filed stories along the way. They reported that the drought had "brought that part of southwestern Saskatchewan ... down to the lowest common denominator."[10]

The Aneroid Co-op was one of the first casualties of the Great Depression. Baker had routinely extended credit to association members, and when these overdue accounts went unpaid, the store went bankrupt. After years of helping others, Everett had to swallow his pride and apply for assistance from the Saskatchewan Relief Commission in November 1931.

The Bakers, with their son, Bill, and adopted daughter, Joan, somehow managed to survive these bleak years, as did many Saskatchewan families during the Dirty Thirties. But the desperate times did nothing to dampen

Everett's unbridled enthusiasm for the co-operative spirit. If anything, the hardship and deprivation experienced by his family and neighbours made co-operation more relevant than it ever had been. He also continued to do his part to help realize that ideal by signing on as an organizer for the Saskatchewan Poultry Pool in 1935. It was exactly the kind of marketing strategy, he likely believed, that would help put the province back on its economic feet.[11]

JOINING THE SASKATCHEWAN WHEAT POOL

Baker's co-operative beliefs and his special ability to communicate those beliefs were rewarded in 1937 when he was hired as a field man for the Saskatchewan Wheat Pool. The once-mighty Wheat Pool had come close to collapse at the start of the Depression, but was bailed out by the federal government on the condition that it stop selling wheat and simply continue as a co-operative elevator company. The Wheat Pool, however, was not satisfied with simply handling grain, so in keeping with its origins, it promoted co-operative education and the creation of other co-operative ventures through its Field Service Division.

The people at the forefront of this activity, more commonly known today as "outreach," were the Pool field staff or what one historian has called "missionaries of rural development."[12] Assigned a district and equipped with a car, these hand-picked men moved from town to town, extolling the virtues of co-operation and organizing new co-ops, from stores to credit unions to insurance. They also sponsored co-operative workshops, sold subscriptions to the Pool newspaper, *The Western Producer*, and signed up new members to the various co-operative or Pool groups. They served as troubleshooters and prided themselves on solving local problems. Baker could not have written a better job description for himself.[13]

In 1937, Everett moved with his family to North Battleford to take up his duties as Wheat Pool field man for District 16 in west-central Saskatchewan.[14] If they had expected to escape from the heavy hand of the drought, they would have been disappointed. That was the year the drought extended its reach to the North Saskatchewan country, with devastating consequences for agriculture. Provincial wheat production dropped to a stunning thirty-five million bushels, a paltry 2.5 bushels per acre. It was the smallest harvest in thirty years, the major difference being that the 1908 crop had been grown on less than twenty percent of the 1937 acreage.[15]

These kinds of setbacks made the field men's visits all the more important to the farming communities they served. In an effort to lift the burden of the Depression, if only for a few hours, they arrived at rural schoolhouses armed with a small projector, a clutch of car batteries, and several films from the growing Wheat Pool collection. Once the portable electricity had been hooked up, they provided an evening's entertainment to overflow audiences. Cartoons, dramas, and documentaries were intermixed with running comments about the Wheat Pool and other co-operative topics. By the end of the 1930s, field men were hosting about seven hundred film nights a year, a phenomenon that is remembered with affection to this day. Equally important, the picture shows created a popular following for the Pool field men in rural Saskatchewan and, in doing so, greatly facilitated their co-operative work.[16]

Everett Baker stepped into his new role with relative ease. He had always been a talker and his unstinting faith in co-operatives gave his presentations a real flair. As his friend Tilly Wilkins later recalled, "His head was always in the clouds planning another co-operative or something."[17] He was never aggressive or argumentative as a field man, but won over people with his selfless, gentlemanly style.[18] He also had a penchant for organization and soon developed an annual breakdown of how many days field men should be devoting to various activities—such as sixty days for film nights.[19] What made his work unique among field men, however, were his slide shows on the co-operative movement and what it meant to the lives of the people of rural Saskatchewan. And it all stemmed from his chance purchase of a camera from one of the first refugees of the European descent into war.

PHOTOGRAPHING AN ERA

In September 1938, Great Britain handed over the Sudetenland, part of western Czechoslovakia, to Nazi Germany under the terms of the controversial 1938 Munich Agreement. The cession of the territory was the cost of appeasing fascist dictator Adolf Hitler, who had threatened to invade Czechoslovakia. But the agreement, which was supposed to guarantee "peace in our time," effectively doomed thousands of anti-Nazi Germans residing in the Sudetenland, who

4285. Sudeten refugees, Makwa, 1940.

literally fled before the occupying Nazi forces. "They left by the back door," Baker later quipped, "when Hitler came in the front door."[20]

In response, the British government not only offered the refugees temporary asylum, but worked with Canada to settle several hundred families in Saskatchewan and British Columbia. The Saskatchewan-bound Sudetens, who had been placed under the care of Canadian National Railways (CNR), arrived throughout the spring and summer of 1939 at rail's end at St. Walburg. They were temporarily housed in boxcars before taking up their land to the north in the Brightsand, Goodsoil, and Loon Lake areas.[21]

That is where Baker met some of them in July 1939 during a visit to the region. According to an upbeat article Baker wrote about the experience in *The Western Producer*, he found the Sudeten settlers cheerfully going about their chores clearing the land and building homes. "There's a sense of release, of new opportunity," he reported, "and a friendly handclasp easily touches off a smile."[22] He also noted that several families had already started a pork ring and that co-operation was their best defence against failure.

What Everett downplayed in his article, however, was their general lack of any farming experience. Most of the Sudeten Germans were skilled tradesmen and factory workers, and did not know how to care for animals, let alone use a plough. They were also placed on poor land that the CNR had purchased at rock-bottom prices from farmers who themselves had failed. To make matters worse, much of the promised equipment and provisions was either old or inadequate.[23] The refugees' first few years in Canada were consequently ones of hardship and deprivation. "Conditions are terrible among them," wrote a visitor to the St. Walburg settlement in 1940. "Most of them have practically nothing to eat … it is the worst misery and poverty I have seen."[24]

This destitution helps explain why Hugo Haas, a former timber merchant with a wife (Margarete), two sons (Herbert and Gabriel), and a nephew (Kurt), was willing, albeit with some reluctance, to part with his Leica camera.[25] Even though it was probably one of the few possessions he managed to spirit out of the Sudetenland, Haas needed the money to help his family as they struggled to meet the challenge of starting a new home in the bush near Loon Lake (what was then known as South Makwa).

Baker, on the other hand, was drawn to the plight of the refugees and followed their progress with great interest and concern. He wrote letters on

3484. Projector used by field men, Kenosee Lake, 1946.

their behalf, decrying the need for more adequate support, and organized donation drives for clothing and other items.[26]

Baker's reasons for purchasing Haas's camera, however, can only be speculated about since he had never expressed an interest in photography up to then and yet paid one hundred dollars for the machine. Given his generous nature, it is quite likely that Baker saw it as a way of helping an immigrant family in distress without causing them any embarrassment. At the same time, the camera would be an invaluable addition to his field equipment. He could use the Leica, loaded with the new Kodachrome film (first introduced in 1935), to create slide presentations to illustrate his field talks and supplement his film offerings on picture show nights.[27] According to former co-worker Alice Allen, Baker had a profound liking for the landscape on the edge of the boreal forest in the province and was keen to use a good camera to capture its scenic beauty.[28]

With camera in hand, the forty-six-year-old Baker set out to photograph the co-operative movement. He could not have chosen a better time to document its "triumphal stage."[29] The period from 1940 to 1960 was the heyday of co-operatives in Saskatchewan—from the revitalized Wheat Pool to larger, more powerful consumer co-operatives to the mushrooming number of credit unions. Everett took pictures of co-op stores, co-op schools, co-op conventions, new credit unions, and Wheat Pool elevator additions. He literally photographed anything with a co-op label or co-op sign.

But he did not stop there. During his long days on the road, travelling from one meeting to another, Baker used his camera to capture the diverse Saskatchewan landscape through the seasons. "He would see a rainbow, stop driving, and spend an immense time taking pictures, just right, miss the time he should be somewhere," remembered Art Force of Shaunavon. "Everett could see beauty where no one else could."[30] These diversions meant that he was always running late, usually for supper, but his wife, Ruth, just took it in stride.[31]

Baker also coaxed people, from kids to the elderly to young families, to pose for him, whether it be in front of their home, in their garden or field, or along the main street or outside a store. What is most striking about these images, apart from the richness of their colour and the skilful use of light, are the happy, smiling faces: people seemingly brimming with a quiet pride that

Baker wanted to take their photograph. Many who posed for him were rewarded with a few complimentary slides that he often sent as a thank you. And according to Jim Forrest, one of the last surviving Wheat Pool field men, people "worshipped" him for this kindly gesture.[32]

Baker's slides became the standard feature of his presentations. His talks were something of an event, known not only for the marvellous colour pictures but the engaging commentary. But like all virtuoso performances, they required meticulous preparation and practice—from dating, labelling, eliminating, and organizing the slides to preparing the script. "People who think they can take a strange set of pictures and run them with no prepared comment," Baker once observed, "will ordinarily ruin the show."[33]

The slide shows were also a novelty, a much-anticipated treat when entertainment was a scarce commodity. A future commissioner of the Royal Canadian Mounted Police claimed that he saw colour photography for the first time as a ten-year-old during one of Baker's presentations at the Keatley school. "As I am sure you know," he fondly told Baker many years later, "my parents and all of us 'young uns' used to look forward to your visits and all the stimulating conversation that used to flow there from."[34] This heartfelt appreciation is understandable. Much of rural Saskatchewan at the time, including most towns and villages, lacked electricity and indoor toilets, in addition to many other modern conveniences that people in urban centres took for granted.

That is one of the reasons why Baker's photographs are so significant today. He was documenting a Saskatchewan that was out of step with the urban, modern, affluent world of the late 1940s and especially the 1950s. The symbol of this new, prosperous Canada was the white, middle-class, two-parent family, living in a new housing division in the suburbs, where the husband was the breadwinner and his wife stayed at home and raised their children. It was also a consumer-driven society, bent on reaping the rewards of prosperity, whether it be a new home or car; the latest gadget on the market, such as a television set; or more leisure time with the family. There was also greater opportunity, made possible largely because of improved access to better education and training, especially at the post-secondary level. Saskatchewan, by contrast, was a much different place, the product of a much different ideal. Seven out of every ten citizens still lived in a rural setting in

1951. In fact, the province remained essentially rural in identity and outlook until the end of the 1960s.[35]

Baker's photographing of provincial life in the 1940s and 1950s was also timely in that rural Saskatchewan was on the cusp of fundamental change. These years may have been the golden age of co-operatives, but the widespread adoption of farm machinery after the Second World War and the movement to larger holdings had accelerated the pace of rural depopulation. Agriculture, meanwhile, was beset with instability. The most troubling development, however, was the fact that the province had to find its way in a new post-war world where rural life was seen as backward, lacking in opportunity, but worst of all, in decline. "Saskatchewan," wrote Nipawin-born writer Sharon Butala, "was only a holding area where one waited impatiently till one was old enough to leave in order to enter the excitement of the real world."[36]

Faced with this steady out-migration, the Co-operative Commonwealth Federation (CCF) government of Tommy Douglas (1944–1961) chose to take Saskatchewan down the road to modernity by providing rural folk with the same level of service and quality of life as their urban counterparts. It closed hundreds of one-room schools, constructed a province-wide system of all-weather grid roads, expanded and upgraded the provincial telephone system, and provided financial assistance to install sewage and water systems. The CCF's most ambitious revitalization program, however, was the provision of electricity to fifty thousand farms and all towns and villages in the province by the end of the 1950s. These modernization efforts may not have stopped rural depopulation as the Douglas government hoped, but they did much to improve the quality of rural life. They signalled a changing rural Saskatchewan, one increasingly different from the place photographed by Baker at the beginning of the modernization process.[37]

A PASSION FOR HISTORY

The sense that Saskatchewan was undergoing a major transformation probably accounted for Baker's other great passion apart from co-operatives and photography—his interest in the province's history. When he moved with his family to North Battleford to take up his field man duties in 1937, he found himself living across the North Saskatchewan River from the old territorial capital and former headquarters of the North-West Mounted Police. He also likely heard stories of how half a century earlier, the residents of Battleford had come under siege within the walls of the police stockade during the 1885 North-West Rebellion and that eight Indian warriors were hanged en masse at the barracks. Even more intriguing was the fact that the Indian bands that were held responsible for the troubles were on his doorstep, still residing on several reserves in the Battlefords area. His frequent trips to the northwest also brought him into contact with Barr Colonists, a group of English immigrants who had established Lloydminster at the beginning of the twentieth century, as well as First Nations and Métis peoples who had been involved in the rebellion along the North Saskatchewan.

Baker not only began to photograph local Aboriginal people, but started collecting information about the rebellion. He personally visited the sites of all the 1885 engagements, often calling on local people living nearby for directions, and tried to figure out exactly where events had taken place. He was helped in this work by Aboriginal elders who had some direct connection to the rebellion, such as Métis Charlie Trottier of Loon Lake who was twenty when he fought at Batoche. Baker also read contemporary accounts of the battles and tried to visualize the scene in 1885 while standing in the same place. "You can't read history and understand it with anything like completeness," he maintained, "unless you visit the sites and travel the trails."[38]

Baker published the results of his investigations in a 1950 article in the journal *Saskatchewan History*. He complained that the rebellion sites had been largely neglected, if not forgotten. "Fort Pitt," he declared, "furnishes the outstanding example of almost complete indifference to history." (It was once the most important fur trade community between forts Carlton and Edmonton.) What was even more irksome was the placement of historical cairns—the ones for Fish Creek and Cutknife Hill were in the wrong place, not even near the actual sites of the battles. "One could wish," he sarcastically observed, "there might be markers ... where events occurred."[39]

In 1945, Everett was transferred to Wheat Pool headquarters in Regina to serve as a kind of official photographer for the Country Organization Department. His slide shows had proven a surefire way of getting "local colour" into his programs, so the Wheat Pool decided to send him into other Pool districts ostensibly for the same purpose. He would shoot a series of slide pictures and then turn them over to the local field men to incorporate into their talks.[40] The CCF government, under the auspices of a new Department of Co-operation and Co-operative Development, was also in the process of establishing a series of large co-operative farms for young veterans and their families, and Baker was called upon to document the early days of the initiative on film.[41]

These various assignments took him to other parts of the province, as well as enabled him to spend more time pursuing his growing interest in the province's history. In 1947, for example, he arranged for W. B. Cameron, a survivor of the April 1885 Frog Lake massacre, to return to the Lloydminster area to revisit some of the rebellion sites. But both Baker and the Pool soon concluded that he was needed more as a field man, and in 1948, he rejoined the field staff, this time based in Shaunavon (district 3), near the eastern edge of the Cypress Hills and about one hundred kilometres west of his former home at Aneroid.

Everett resumed his field service duties with the same energy and commitment that he first brought to the position. He never seemed to tire or lose faith in what he was doing. In one year alone, he spent 288 days on the road, covering nearly 20,000 miles.[42] Baker's new posting in the southwest was reflected in his photography, which now included scenes of the rolling, open range country and the people and events of the local ranching industry—roundups, cattle auctions, calf shows, rodeos.[43]

He was also drawn to the region's history and its stories: how the North-West Mounted Police had once patrolled the isolated border country on horseback, or how Lakota Sioux Chief Sitting Bull and his warriors had sought refuge in the Wood Mountain area following their annihilation of the American 7th Cavalry at the Battle of the Little Big Horn in 1876. "I was inoculated," he later recounted, "by hearing discussions and seeing bits of ... trail here and there."[44] As he had done during his rebellion research, he liked to "turn the clock back" and pretend that he was seeing the land as others before him—Indians, Mounties, ranchers, and homesteaders—had known it.

THE SASKATCHEWAN HISTORY & FOLKLORE SOCIETY

By the early 1950s, Everett was deeply involved in local community and heritage issues. When the provincial government established the Royal Commission on Agriculture and Rural Life to seek advice on how best to secure

7528. Sonja Lidfors with NWMP trail marker, 1960.

the future of rural Saskatchewan, Baker helped facilitate several community forums and provided input himself.[45] He also served on the subcommittee charged with identifying historical sites as part of the province's diamond jubilee celebrations in 1955. That same year, Baker self-published *Trails and Traces of Rupert's Land and the North-West Territories as seen from 1940-1955*, a collection of colour photographs largely concerned with his field research into late nineteenth-century Saskatchewan history. In his preface, he spoke about his plans to produce future picture stories in the interests of compiling a more comprehensive record of the province's early days.[46]

This goal led to Baker's involvement in the founding of the Saskatchewan History & Folklore Society (SHFS). Many people interested in the province's past had been energized by the jubilee celebrations and wanted to build on the momentum generated by the spate of community histories and other anniversary activities before it was lost. To that end, Blodwen Davies, executive secretary of the Saskatchewan Arts Board, along with Dr. Richard Johnson, a University of Toronto professor gathering folk music in the province, called a meeting in Fort Qu'Appelle in August 1957 to discuss the creation of a Saskatchewan folklore committee. Everett and Ruth Baker were among the two dozen invited delegates.

The recorded minutes of the meeting communicated a sense of urgency. Mrs. M. K. Edwards of Melfort spoke for many when she expressed alarm about "how much is passing." But the delegates were divided on whether the new organization should be a history or folklore committee. Dr. Johnson observed, "History frightens a lot of people away ... history has a habit of becoming dull when it gets into the hands of certain unimaginative people ... but history is actually lore."[47] It was eventually decided to strike a series of subcommittees representing the varied interests—such as folk dance, folk tales, personal histories, Indian lore, and bibliography—and convene another meeting that fall. One of the last items of business was Baker's selection as president by acclamation.

At the next meeting in Regina in early November, Baker proposed a new name for the committee, the Saskatchewan History & Folklore Society, that would better reflect the dual interests of the group. He noted, "One reason for a little more emphasis on Saskatchewan history is that ... there hasn't been enough of it." He also pushed for a formal constitution. "I'm for a permanent organization," he declared in his chairman's remarks, "because there are jobs to do that no one else is doing—jobs that won't be done, unless they are done very soon."[48] The meeting then endorsed a set of key objectives, including the collection of Saskatchewan folk songs; the marking of historic sites and trails; the organization of conducted tours, annual conferences, and special publications; and greater promotion of history and folklore in Saskatchewan schools. The bus tours, which have become a hallmark of the SHFS today, may have had their origin in co-operative study tours first organized by the Wheat Pool in the late 1940s.

Baker had assumed the presidency of the SHFS with the knowledge that his days as a field man would come to an end with his retirement in January 1958. But at the last minute the Wheat Pool asked him to stay on for another five months to help with a special egg marketing campaign. He welcomed the extra paycheques, but not the extra work, especially when he had just been recruited by his friend J. D. Herbert at the Calgary-based Glenbow Foundation to do historical field research in southwestern Saskatchewan.

The sixty-five-year-old Baker consequently spent the first part of 1958 juggling three jobs, including nursing along the fledgling SHFS. He was reluctant to give up his new Glenbow duties, particularly when the work nicely complemented the SHFS mandate and fed his interest in the region's history and photography. Baker filed monthly reports to the Glenbow throughout the summer and fall of 1958, on such places as Fort Walsh and Sitting Bull's camp, before devoting the winter to sorting through the material he had collected during his twenty-one-year career with the Pool. The following spring, his Glenbow duties were terminated when the research director he was working for abruptly resigned.[49] His release left him free to tackle a major new project.

The other hat that Baker wore at the SHFS was convener of the Historic Sites and Trails committee. And in 1959, probably as a direct result of his recent historical work for the Glenbow, he launched an ambitious campaign to mark the old North-West Mounted Police (NWMP) trail from Wood Mountain to Fort Walsh, the major thoroughfare in southwestern Saskatchewan in the late nineteenth century. As Baker told Allan Turner of the Saskatchewan Archives Board, the commemoration "cannot be done at all if delayed a short time longer."[50] Part of the challenge was determining the exact route of the 190-mile trail. Here, Baker depended on old surveyors' maps, the memories of pioneer homesteaders and ranchers, and a team of dedicated local volunteers (Boyd Anderson, Rube Freel, Russell Flynn, and Reddy Parsonage, among others) who took responsibility for locating certain sections of the trail. It was painstaking work, as evidenced by the extremely detailed colour-coded notes in Baker's papers, and of course, the photographs that accompanied the research on the ground. He also called on the Royal Canadian Mounted Police for whatever assistance they could offer. Former Commissioner S. T. Wood even wanted to pitch in.[51]

The other major challenge was funding the project, in particular paying for the 260 concrete posts and cast aluminum plates that would mark the trail. In many instances, Baker would simply drop in on friends and tell them that he was trying to save the trail in the hope that they would make a contribution. One such visit to a Bracken farmer working in his field netted a cheque for one hundred dollars. On another occasion, he talked an old timer, who originally planned to support the project in his will, into turning over the cash then and there. "Do you know we could make a lot better use of that thousand now," Baker told the donor, "than to wait until you're dead."[52]

Baker also continued to give picture shows and then canvas the audience for donations at the end of the program. The money collected never met the initial needs of the project, and Baker had to cover some of the expenses himself so that the work could proceed. But in the end he raised over ten thousand dollars, most of it from individuals who appreciated what was being done in the name of history. "There's the old trail," remarked Wallace Cameron, whose parents had homesteaded in the Mankota area. "We've marked it just in time. Now it carries us into the future."[53] The project was featured in the July 1961 edition of the *RCMP Quarterly* and included Baker's photograph of a laughing, young girl holding a trail nameplate on the front cover.[54] The trail project also earned Baker an award of merit in 1963 from the American Association for State and Local History.[55]

Everett had ambitious plans to mark other historic Saskatchewan trails, but finding the funds proved a deterrent. He kept busy though, even after he stepped down as president of the SHFS in 1963. "I couldn't see any point in retiring from this world," he told a friend, "and have continued here [Shaunavon] ... with never a dull moment ... preserving the old Sask. and NWT history before it slips through our fingers and is lost."[56]

He worked on various restoration projects, including the old NWMP post at Wood Mountain and Chimney Coulee in the Cypress Hills, with the assistance of Lakota Sioux John Okute-sica (LeCaine) and George Shepherd, curator of the Western Development Museum and a former resident of the area. He also regularly accompanied his friend Corky Jones of Eastend to the Badlands to search for dinosaur bones and looked forward to the day when a new Grasslands national park would perhaps be set aside near Val Marie.[57] All of these outings were recorded on slide film and incorporated into the picture shows that were still in great demand.

By the late 1960s, Baker had come to believe that "the most important part of my mission in life is still ahead."[58] He regularly wrote letters to newspapers decrying the evils of alcohol. He was also an outspoken critic of American military involvement in Vietnam, mockingly calling for a new motto, "in violence we trust." He even suggested that social engineering should go hand in hand with the advances in mechanical engineering.

It was also around this time that Everett looked into becoming a Canadian citizen. He and his wife, Ruth, both landed immigrants who had lost their American citizenship when they voted in a municipal election, had spurned the idea as long as it involved swearing allegiance to the Crown. He now wondered whether it would be possible for them to secure citizenship without the necessary oath. "We have a real affection for Canada and for Canadian neighbors developed over an acquaintance of over 50 years," he wrote the Trudeau government. "They have been very kind."[59] The matter would never be resolved.

In 1972, Baker was the subject of a front page story, "In on ground floor of history," in *Co-operative Consumer* magazine. The reporter found the seventy-nine-year-old former Pool field man, with poor eyesight, sitting in his Shaunavon home office, surrounded by his slides, books, clippings, and manuscripts. "If his brain were as cluttered as his office," read the article's opening sentence, "Everett Baker would wake up every morning with a headache, go to sleep with a migraine, and have very interesting dreams."[60] The article then went on to provide a brief account of his career and how he still had a good deal of intellectual fight in him. Failing health, however, soon forced the Bakers to move into a retirement home. Everett died in 1981. He was buried in Swift Current in the prairie soil he loved.

TRIBUTE

In 1984, Baker was posthumously recognized with the Saskatchewan Co-operative Merit Award. It was a fitting tribute to someone who had devoted the better part of his life to the co-operative movement in the province. But Baker also left his own legacy, a one-of-a-kind gift to his adopted Saskatchewan. In January 1981, only three months before his death, he proudly turned over nearly ten thousand slides to the Co-operative College of Canada to serve as a teaching tool, much as he had once used them during his days as a field man. But no one ever showed any interest in the slides until Finn Andersen, executive director of the Saskatchewan History & Folklore Society, inquired about their existence as part of the society's fortieth anniversary celebrations. The college gladly turned over the unique collection in June 1997.

Since then, the colour slides have been used by the SHFS to educate and entertain thousands of people about Everett Baker's world: the co-operative movement in all its forms; the province's rich and exciting history; and the individuals, places, and events along the way that made his life such an interesting and fulfilling journey. In retrospect, Saskatchewan is fortunate that Everett Baker bought that Leica camera. His photographic documentation of the province in the mid-twentieth century is a national treasure.

BILL WAISER, SASKATOON
2007

EVERETT BAKER'S SASKATCHEWAN

A NOTE ABOUT THE CAPTIONS

The following images were selected from the almost ten thousand original slide photographs held by the Saskatchewan History & Folklore Society (SHFS) in its Regina office. They represent a small sample of the rich Baker collection. Everett Baker printed a brief note, including the location and date the photo was taken, around the edge of every slide. These original notations—in Baker's own words— have been used to caption the photographs. Some of the names may be spelled incorrectly. The slide numbers (bottom left) were assigned by the SHFS after its acquisition of the Baker collection.

29. Carl Klein's variety test plot, Admiral, 1953.

56. Mrs. John Joffle and Mrs. Norene Wigness, Jubilee parade, Admiral, 1955.

75. Orma McDonough and Norman Wilson wedding, Admiral, 1951.

80. Ed Faber (Pool elevator agent), George Farnworth (Co-op Store) and Harry Wickerstrom (Livestock and Co-op Oil), Admiral, 1948.

131. Co-op Store, Algrove, 1946.

141. Wellington Simpson (manager), Walter Linton, and Mark Corbin, Co-op gas station, Aneroid, 1948.

148. Haidi Ruchs cuts ribbon at opening of new elevator annex, Aneroid, 1955.

160. Electing officers at Quimper school co-op, Aneroid, 1949.

188. Unloading shoots at Calf Club Show and Sale, Aneriod, 1949.

190. Line-up, Calf Club Show and Sale, Aneroid, 1949.

231. Car license plate at Jubilee parade, Aneroid, 1955.

339. Ukrainian Catholic church, Arran, 1949.

367. Oldtimers and old times with Charlie Trottier, Batoche, 1948.

375. Eva M. Gaff home, Battle Creek, 1960.

396. Taking leave of the fish filleting staff, Beaver Lake, 1946.

518. Main street, Bracken, 1942.

536. Bracken Co-op picnic, 1950.

520. Children racing at Co-op picnic, Bracken, 1950.

583. Moeckl's old Manson cabin, Brightsand, 1944.

613. Pool elevator agents, Cadillac, 1951.

640. Mr. and Mrs. Anderson, Co-op oil couple, Cadillac, 1946.

642. Mr. and Mrs. George Smith, Cadillac, 1953.

643. Wernicke family and garden, Cadillac, 1954.

650. Citizenship Day, Cadillac high school, 1952.

685. Lone Tree branding, Canuck, 1957.

744. Lone Tree bookkeeper, Canuck, 1957.

815. Fairview street, Co-op construction camp, Carrot River, 1949.

828. Children in Co-op farm construction camp, Carrot River, 1949.

6912. Carl Jackson standing in barley field, Chambery, 1956.

920. Arnold Schmidt feeding calves, Claydon, 1956.

926. Mrs. Donald McLeod, Claydon, 1956.

1013. 951 cattle sold at livestock sale, Climax, 1957.

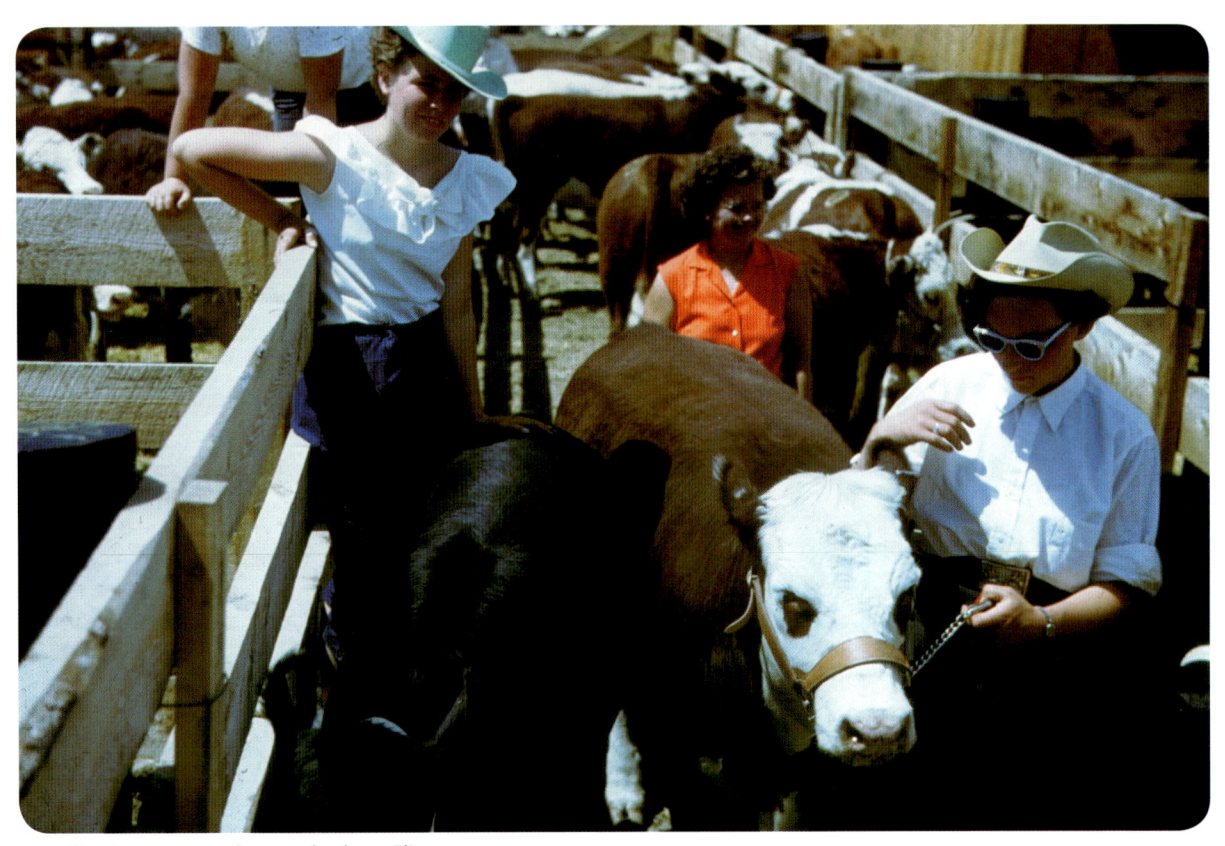

1077. Bracken 4-H members and calves, Climax, 1957.

1079. Gordon Smith at 4-H show, Climax, 1957.

EVERETT BAKER'S SASKATCHEWAN

1097. Main street, Climax, 1951.

1138. At Climax 4-H Calf Club, 1956.

1165. Stone pile crossing on the Whitemud, Climax, 1956.

1145. Miss Robinson and primary class, Climax, 1951.

1208. Willet's ranch north of Climax, Whitemud valley, 1951.

1317. Soil survey dinner, Compass, 1944.

1333. Paying the prizes, Calf Club show, Consul, 1949.

1381. Bob Frances' race horse, Crichton, 1950.

1383. Cy Matthew's family, Crichton, 1957.

1384. Boys at Crichton Pool elevator, 1957.

1395. Poundmaker picture and relatives, Cut Knife, 1942.

1413. Gabriel Lavallie and son Joe, Cypress Hills, 1948.

1451. Debden dairy pool cheese factory transport (forest fire smoke in background), 1950.

1529. George, Peter, Nancy, and Mrs. Butala, Divide, 1953.

1554. Stories being told at International picnic, Divide, 1953.

1576. The Darling Family, Divide, 1952.

1603. A. Allemand home, Dollard, 1951.

1620. Row boat south of Dollard, 1958.

1717. Sweat house frames near 1941 pow wow tents, Dorintosh.

1735. St. Laurent pilgrimage, Duck Lake, 1944.

1747. Fat crackles for lunch, St. Laurent pilgrimage, Duck Lake, 1944.

1750. Indian women digging clay for outside plastering, Duck Lake, 1945.

1850. Calf Club Show and Sale, Eastend, 1949.

1853. Officials and auctioneers stand, Fat Stock Show and Sale, Eastend, 1949.

1908. D. J. McCuaig's new combine, Eastend, 1942.

1948. RCMP at international 4-H rally, Eastend, 1956.

1961. International 4-H clubs having ice cream, Eastend, 1952.

2135. Ben Rose, Eastend, 1951.

2200. Children on platform, Eastend, 1954.

2219. Raymond and Gail White, pin cherries and chokecherries, Eastend, 1952.

2444. Swimming in the Frenchman, Eastend, 1956.

2730. Picnic at Malcolm McTaggart's, Ferland, 1949.

2872. Overlooking Fort Qu'Appelle from cemetery, 1956.

2845. Ceremonial head dress from the rear, Sioux pow wow, Fort Qu'Appelle, 1957.

3000. Ferry crossing, North Saskatchewan, Frenchman Butte, 1941.

2969. Mail day at Frenchman Butte, 1944.

2984. Autumn on the North Saskatchewan from hills southeast of Frenchman Butte, 1947.

3059. Mrs. Sig Skogstad and plums, Frontier, 1952.

3116. Boy Scout swimming hole, Garden Head, 1958.

3141. Heavy rain and rainbow south of Glentworth, 1954.

3183. The Vernon Martin's, Gouverneur, 1956.

3270. Matt Brown and Chet Closs, Gravelbourg, 1947.

1366. Rabbits being hung at the Stonehackers, Greig Lake, 1941.

3334. Customers and staff, Hazenmore Co-op store, 1951.

3357. Mrs. Joe Schaefer and Margaret in hollyhocks, Hazenmore, 1953.

3358. David and Elved Hughes playing in the garden, Hazenmore, 1955.

3389. Looking west-southwest from hotel, Hudson Bay, 1949.

3395. Indians from Barrows, Manitoba, camped near Hudson Bay, 1955.

3443. Dorothy Rust, Instow, 1952.

3444. Shoveling grasshopper sawdust, Instow, 1947.

3149. Northern lake fish, Island Lake, 1945.

3487. Tobogganing under difficulties, Youth training school, Kenosee Lake, 1946.

3497. Youth training school, Kenosee Lake, 1946.

3561. Rock Creek canyon, Killdeer, 1942.

3604. In Don Turgeon's variety test plot, Kincaid, 1950.

3663. Mrs. Percy Lewis and Klintonel post office, 1954.

3966. Cyril Mahoney, fish trapper, La Ronge, 1946.

4007. Mrs. Irwin Studer and Mary Lynn, Lac Pelletier, 1950.

4018. Wedding reception, Irwin Studer home, Lac Pelletier, 1955.

4019. Decoration car for Dennis and Anne Studer, Lac Pelletier, 1955.

4031. Fishing perch at sunset, Lac Pelletier, 1950.

4043. Front of Lashburn Co-op store, 1949.

4051. Stations of the Cross, Liberty, 1946.

4061. Demonstrating hitch farm machinery, Field Day, Liberty, 1946.

4087. Lloydminster, 1942.

4133. Loon Lake Co-op store, 1941.

4152. A. H. Neilly, storekeeper, and Dottie Charlton on Saskatoon settlement road, Loon Lake, 1944.

4154. Indian dog house, Loon Lake, 1943.

4155. Frying bannock, Loon Lake, 1943.

4232. Commercial fishing, Loon Lake, 1944.

4284. Edmund Rohac (on binder), Makwa, 1940.

4318. Nora Way, Mankota, 1948.

4331. Well-tanned shirtless section crew building stockyards, Mankota, 1957.

4339. First commercial livestock sale (530 head sold), Mankota, 1957.

4470. John Olson at Maple Creek stockyards, 1960.

4501. Calf roping at Murraydale rodeo, Maple Creek, 1959.

4523. Girls watching Murraydale rodeo, Maple Creek, 1959.

3768. Co-op school boys at Matador, 1950.

3885. Premier Douglas (far right) and part of his cabinet, Matador, 1947.

3892. Inside new granary, Matador, 1951.

4646. The Alfred Munford's, McCord, 1954.

4700. McCord school, 1951.

4713. Patsy Fewing, McCord, 1957.

4717. Donald, Dale, and Lorne Belcher and Linda Jackson, McCord, 1957.

4775. Melfort Co-op store window, 1946.

4804. Melfort, looking southeast, 1946.

4844. Fields of rape at Laurel co-op farm, Meskanaw, 1949.

4864. Pool elevator and annex official opening, Meyronne, 1951.

4961. "Ladies from Hell" Moose Jaw military parade, 1951.

4969. Girls working in Saskatchewan Wood Products, Moose Jaw, 1946.

5102. Farmer to shipper—advance notice by phone, North Battleford, 1946.

5166. Indian rendezvous, the day after the fair, North Battleford, 1945.

5215. Harvest crew, Bench Hutterite Colony, North Fork, 1960.

5245. 230-pound pumpkin, North Fork, 1954.

EVERETT BAKER'S SASKATCHEWAN

5254. Hutterite children in the alfalfa, North Fork, 1954.

5273. Mrs. Frank Leducer, Onion Lake, 1946.

5371. Cabin, Peck Lake, 1965.

5435. Francis and Edna Mahon, grand champ reserve champ, Calf Show and Sale, Ponteix, 1948.

5440. "I wish she wasn't sold," Calf Show and Sale, Ponteix, 1948.

5455. Ponteix hospital, convent, and church, 1951.

5466. Official opening of new composite Pool elevator, Ponteix, 1956.

5497. Prince Albert horse-drawn dairy pool delivery, 1946.

5575. Mr. and Mrs. Angus McKay, Prince Albert, 1950.

5600. Icing export pork from Burns, Prince Albert, 1944.

5623. Ryott Barroby in variety test plot, Ravenscrag, 1955.

5654. Carleton family, Ravenscrag, 1956.

5655. Kealey Springs school north of Ravenscrag, 1948.

5656. The Maurice Gallot's, Ravenscrag, 1949.

5671. Roy Barroby kids enjoying Whitemud Valley, Ravenscrag, 1955.

5883. Armistice day, Victoria Avenue, Regina, 1941.

5936. Paper declaring "Victory" held by George Baker of Regina, 1945.

5887. V. E. Day from Co-op grocery building at 11th Avenue, Regina, 1945.

5918. Minister of Education Woodrow S. Lloyd and Mrs. Lloyd, Regina, 1947.

6045. The H. E. Sampson eight-seater shell, Regina boat club, 1947.

6053. Sailing on Wascana Lake, Regina Boat Club Day, 1947.

6205. Cattle in the pasture at Ab Smith's, Reliance, 1957.

6248. Winter scene with Bert Sayers family, Reliance, 1957.

6298. Mr. and Mrs. W. K. Nielsen with turkeys, Robsart, 1953.

6394. Students at Rosefield school, 1951.

6439. Swift Current Co-op School en route to Matador Co-op farm, Saskatchewan Landing, 1949.

6493. Saskatoon Co-op wholesale building, 1944.

6461. Saskatoon Co-op store and staff, 1941.

6510. Federated Co-operatives Limited Annual Meeting, Saskatoon, 1963.

6636. Native presentation at Pionera, Saskatoon, 1955.

6765. President Wallie Wilkins at Co-op service station opening, Shaunavon, 1957.

7033. Dynneson girls, Shaunavon fair, 1955.

EVERETT BAKER'S SASKATCHEWAN

7159. Harris Rock in Native costume, Shaunavon Jubilee, 1963.

7332. Grand Challenge Winners, Shaunavon bonspiel, 1949.

7351. Virginia McPhee, Elaine and Sheila Sinclair coming from Creston school on horseback, Shaunavon, 1948.

7367. Sandburn-Duncan wedding party, Shaunavon, 1954.

7443. Mr. and Mrs. Clarence Anderson, Shaunavon, 1952.

7460. Murdie McRae family, Shaunavon, 1957.

7483. Hutterite children, Bench Colony, Shaunavon, 1957.

7492. Oldtimers, Pioneer Hall picnic, Shaunavon, 1947.

7501. Patsy Piechotta, Lillian Lewans, Marlene Ruschkowski, and Agnes Tetzlaff, Pioneer Hall picnic, Shaunavon, 1948.

7518. The Wilbert Lewis family at Blomme picnic, Shaunavon, 1952.

7522. Morley Kolskog Boys, Shaunavon, 1955.

7556. T. J. E. Campbell and sweet peas, Shaunavon, 1951.

7577. Mr. and Mrs. R. P. Robbins in the plum blossoms, Shaunavon, 1954.

9239. Barrett Halderman bike at Shaunavon fair, 1953.

7757. Gayle Cole and colt, South Fork, 1958.

7860. Darlene S. and P-ZZ, South Fork, 1951.

8284. Opening day of stockyards, Co-op producers staff, Swift Current, 1948.

8520. Residents of Sweet Grass reserve, Unity, 1942.

8592. Sisters of Providence, Val Marie, 1954.

8609. Gust Anderson family, Val Marie, 1955.

8618. Restaurant operators, Val Marie, 1954.

8699. Peter Veregin house, Veregin, 1949.

8706. Trains from Humboldt, Prince Albert, and Saskatoon, Wakaw, 1947.

8722. Father Baudoux and Father Ares, Shrine of St. Theresa, Wakaw, 1947.

8746. YWCA tour on *Shamrock*, Waskesiu, 1962.

8761. Indians north of Waterhen bridge, 1940.

8765. Saskatchewan Credit Union Federation 9th annual convention, Watrous, 1947.

8787. Elizabeth Lowery keeps score at ball game during Saskatchewan Credit Union convention, Watrous, 1947.

8949. Wolseley main street, 1946.

8890. Wanbli Sunpagewin (Crossed Eagle Quills), Sitting Bull refugee, Wood Mountain, 1955.

9015. Kelvington Calf Club, Yorkton Fat Stock Show, 1947.

9048. Broadcasting the Yorkton Fat Stock Show, 1947.

APPENDIX

THE LEICA CAMERA AND KODACHROME FILM

by Brock Silversides

Two advancements in photographic technology came together in the 1930s that made possible Everett Baker's wonderfully clear and candid images of Saskatchewan people, places, and events. The first was a camera, the second a film. Together they changed the course of conventional photography, brought it into the modern age, and made it accessible to a larger segment of society.

The first was the development of a pocket-sized, hand-held, "small format" or "miniature format" camera with sharp and interchangeable lenses: the Leica. The term "Leica" itself (much like Kodak) means nothing—it merely combines letters from "Leitz" and "camera" and rolls off the tongue easily. The Leica was designed by Oskar Barnack, chief of research for the Leitz company of Wetzlar, a small city near Hamburg, Germany.

Barnack (1879–1936), director of research and development for the corporation, was himself an avid photographer and mountain climber. Due to asthma, he found it taxing to carry around large view cameras with their accompanying glass plates, especially in the steep hills around Wetzlar. Rather than avoid the hills altogether, Barnack decided to radically alter the concept of the camera instead.[61] While working on a new type of movie camera, he came up with the idea of using 35 mm roll film for still images in a camera that could be carried in one's pocket. In 1913, he constructed a prototype camera that incorporated features now taken for granted.

The Leica was small (52 mm high, 128 mm long, and 28 mm wide). It weighed a mere 430 grams and had the first rangefinder attachment on top (used to accurately aim the camera), a retractable lens of outstanding quality with a wide aperture, a focal plane shutter, variable shutter speeds, a film-advance knob (which also cocked the shutter), and a frame counter. The Leica formed its images as pleasing rectangles measuring 36 x 24 cm (the famous 3 to 2 ratio), and were of such quality as to allow for significant enlargement. Its internal spools initially held fifty frames and later thirty-six. For several years the company motto was "small negatives, large pictures."[62]

Production of the Leica was about to start when the First World War intervened. Four years of hostilities and another five years of depression and reconstruction prevented Leitz from realizing its manufacture. Mass production finally started in 1924, and the first Leica—clad with gold plating and lizard skin—was made available to the public in 1925 at the Liepzig Fair. Leitz had an aggressive marketing team and subsidiaries or contracted vendors on every continent. They sold every unit they could make.

The camera was immediately adopted by professional photojournalists and documentarians like Erich Salomon, Henri Cartier-Bresson, Alexander Rodchenko, and Andre Kertesz. They appreciated its portability, its sturdiness, the rapidity with which consecutive pictures could be taken, and the fact that its small size made the act of photographing less conspicuous. They also liked the idea that they could take a large number of frames without having to reload after each one. The amateur photographic community also embraced the Leica as it did not entail bellows, tripods, dark slides, blackout cloths, or upside down focusing. It was as simple to use as the first amateur camera—the Brownie—but gave noticeably superior results.

By 1930, further improvements had been made to the Leica to include interchangeable lenses, both wide angle and telephoto, and the addition of a photoelectric cell for reading light levels. And if one desired more in-depth information, the American author and publisher Willard Morgan published the definitive guide entitled *The Leica Manual* in 1935, which was periodically revised and updated until the fifteenth edition was published in the early 1970s.

The Leica was slow to be acknowledged in Canada. The first known exhibition, specifically of "Leica Camera Photography," was held on the sixth floor of the Eaton's main store in Toronto in February 1936. Along with 160 images by celebrated German photographer Dr. Paul Wolff, there was an additional feature of 40 photographs by Canadians chosen by the Canadian branch of Leitz. The advertisement for the exhibition read, "Whether you are an amateur photographer, a professional or merely interested, you will find the Exhibition worthy of your attention."[63]

The convenience the Leica afforded was liberating and inspiring, and the number of images being taken increased phenomenally. Within a decade, usage of 35 mm photography equalled that of other larger professional formats, and clearly overtook all previous amateur formats. The Leica continued to be manufactured—although after 1940 it was built with inferior components due to the Leitz plant being commandeered for the Nazi war effort—and used throughout the Second World War by all sides. Robert Capa, Leni Riefenstahl, Yevgeny Khaldei, and Alfred Eisenstaedt were some of the notable war photographers who captured the horrors of the conflict with a Leica.

The perfect partner to the Leica camera was Kodachrome film, itself the culmination of a seventy-five-year quest. From the moment it was introduced to the public in 1839, photography was dogged by one overwhelming demand—the demand for colour images. There had been numerous attempts over the years to make it happen, mostly failures interspersed with a few shining, if impractical, successes. They all fell within the three categories of colour separations, colour screens, and the colour tri-pack.

The Scottish physicist James Clerk Maxwell (1831–79) demonstrated the first known photographic colour image. In 1861, he exposed three separate black and white glass negatives of a multicoloured ribbon. He processed them as positives, projected them on a wall—each one through either a blue, green, or red filter—and superimposed them in register. It was both complicated and crude, but it certainly reproduced a relatively accurate range of colours. Later that decade in France, Louis Ducos du Hauron and Charles Cros, independently of each other, continued research along these lines using red, yellow, and blue filters and odd-looking cameras with three lens barrels.

An early Kodachrome film using two coloured layers was invented in 1913. It exposed two different glass plates through two different filters. Each one was processed as a positive, then bound together in register. The result was muddy and did not give a full rendition of all colours. It was also time-consuming and relatively insensitive, with exposures taking up to ten seconds to register in strong sunlight. It was difficult to get instantaneous or candid pictures with an exposure of that duration.

The next approach to engross researchers was the colour screen processes whereby the image was exposed through tiny, even microscopic, straight or cross-hatched lines or dot-shaped colour filters, visually blended by the viewers' eyes. The most successful of these processes was the Autochrome, invented by Auguste and Louis Lumiere in 1903. Their "film" consisted of a black and white glass negative covered on the reverse side by a screen made up of finely ground red, green, and blue starch grains. The photograph was taken through the screen and the negative reversal processes. The image was in turn viewed back through the same screen. The Autochrome process softly rendered colours, but the "grain" was huge and in many ways resembled a pointillist painting. It was marketed to the public in 1907, but due to its expense it was not widely used in Canada. There were drawbacks too: it was insensitive, requiring long exposures, and it had to be processed by either a professional or an amateur with a far-above-average knowledge of photo chemistry. Other incarnations of the colour screen process included Dufaycolor (by Ilford), Agfacolor, and Finlaycolor.

None of the above processes proved capable of rendering true colour in a continuous tone, and certainly none were particularly welcoming to the amateur photographer. It remained up to the third approach—the integral tri-pack—to accomplish this. The tri-pack contains three layers of emulsions sensitive to the three basic light colours (red, yellow, and blue), which are exposed and viewed as one entity.

It took the efforts of two American musicians, Leopold Mannes and Leopold Godowsky (known to their colleagues as "God" and "man"—a formidable-sounding team), over twenty years to fully realize the concept. They started working on it while still in high school, borrowing money from their parents and carrying out experiments in the bathroom sink. One can only attain a certain level of professionalism with budgets and facilities like these, and so they succumbed to the inevitable. In 1927 they sought out the help of Eastman Kodak. The corporation was impressed with their work, provided them with materials, and finally hired them as full-time researchers. In its early stages, their research was called the "Leica Film Project," as that was the camera they knew their film was most likely going to be used in.[64]

The technology they perfected was known as a tri-pack. In essence it incorporated three different emulsions—magenta, cyan, and yellow—on one piece of 35 mm film. Each layer was processed in a separate step, with chemical dye couplers being added along the way. The entire development consisted of twenty-eight steps lasting three and a half hours, and of course only Kodak could do it. The result was a positive transparency or "slide" that was generally mounted in a small cardboard mat so it could be projected.

Kodachrome exhibited amazingly fine grain, was brighter and sharper, and gave a tonal range that was superior to anything that had gone before. Kodak introduced this first professional/amateur colour film to the world in April 1935 to almost universal acclaim. It was available as both motion picture and still film in 8 mm, 16 mm, and 35 mm gauges. The price for an eighteen exposure roll was $3.50 (US), roughly equal to $30 today and that included processing.[65] It was noticeably expensive when compared to black and white, and was an expenditure to be carefully considered in the 1930s. Sales lagged during the Depression years, but for people like Everett Baker, who was so personally dedicated to colour and driven by his urge to document Saskatchewan, the expense was not hard to justify.

At the beginning, Kodachrome was also relatively insensitive, with a light exposure rating (expressed as ASA/ISO) of 8 in daylight. That was increased over the years to 16 in 1945; 25 in 1961; and 64 in 1962. The bright, clear light of the Saskatchewan skies more than compensated for this shortcoming. Just as the Leica heralded the onset of 35 mm photography, so Kodachrome initiated the massive public switchover from black and white to colour photography.

Finally, for an image made up of colour dyes, Kodachrome has proven itself as one of the most stable, and this is why the Everett Baker images have aged so well. The combination of a dedicated and skilful photographer, an easy-to-use but still high-quality camera, and a long-lasting and brilliant colour film came together to ensure that an important chunk of Saskatchewan's visual history was faithfully recorded for posterity.

Brock Silversides is currently the director of the media commons department of the University of Toronto Libraries. An ex-Saskatchewanian, he has worked as an audio-visual archivist and librarian for over twenty-five years for the Saskatoon Public Library (Local History Room), the Saskatchewan Archives Board, the Provincial Archives of Alberta, The Medicine Hat Museum & Art Gallery, and the National Library of Canada.

Brock's ongoing research interests include western Canadian photography, filmmaking, and music, and he has curated or co-curated thirty exhibitions relating to these areas. He is the author or co-author of twelve books or exhibition catalogues, including *Face Pullers: Photographing Native Canadians 1871–1939*; *Waiting For the Light: Early Mountain Photography in BC and Alberta*; *Prairie Sentinel: The Story of the Canadian Grain Elevator*; *Shooting Cowboys: Photographing Canadian Cowboy Culture 1878–1965*; and *Looking West: Photographing the Canadian Prairies 1858–1957*. Brock's most recent book is *Fort de Prairies: The Story of Fort Edmonton*, written for the 2005 provincial centennial.

NOTES AND FURTHER READING

INTRODUCTION

1. Heather Smith, "Picturing a Utopian Reality," in *Everett Baker: Picturing a Utopian Reality* (Moose Jaw: Moose Jaw Museum and Art Gallery, 2003), 13; Everett Baker interview, 9 November 1970, Saskatchewan Archives Board (SAB).
2. Smith, "Picturing," 13; Baker, interview.
3. Bill Waiser, *Saskatchewan: A New History* (Calgary: Fifth House Publishers, 2005), 256–58.
4. Baker's January 1924 contract with the new Saskatchewan Wheat Pool indicated that he was renting a half-section of land in addition to his own half-section. He had less than 160 acres devoted to wheat in 1922. University of Saskatchewan Archives, Saskatchewan Wheat Pool papers (SWP), Box 2, Everett Baker, Folder 1.
5. Smith, "Picturing," 14–15; Baker, interview.
6. For an examination of Baker's co-operative ideas, see Brett Fairbairn, "Everett Baker and the Culture of Co-operation in Saskatchewan," in *Everett Baker: Picturing a Utopian Reality,* 26–41.
7. Everett Baker, *Working Together: Each for All and All for Each* (Aneroid, SK: Aneroid Co-operative Association, 1930), 5, 60.
8. Waiser, *Saskatchewan*, 266–67.
9. Library and Archives Canada, Manuscript Division, Charlotte Whitton papers, v. 25, "C. W. Report re Unemployment and Relief in Western Canada, 1932," handwritten notes starting 27 June 1932.
10. D. B. Macrae and R. M. Scott, *In the South Country* (Saskatoon: Star-Phoenix, 1934), 13.
11. Smith, "Picturing," 16–17.
12. Ian MacPherson, "Missionaries of Rural Development: The Fieldmen of the Saskatchewan Wheat Pool," *Agricultural History* 60, no. 2 (spring 1986): 76–83.
13. Baker described his role as "developing the ideal co-operative democracy, wherein everyone knows where he and his neighbours are heading for, and takes a personal interest in seeing that they get there." Ibid., 82.
14. The Wheat Pool numbered the sixteen field districts, starting in the bottom, right-hand corner of the province, in the same fashion as the Dominion Lands survey system.
15. Waiser, *Saskatchewan*, 282.
16. MacPherson, "Missionaries," 85–88.
17. Smith, "Picturing," 23.
18. Barrett Halderman, interview by author, 21 June 2006.
19. MacPherson, "Missionaries," 89–90.
20. Baker, interview.
21. Jonathon Wagner, "Saskatchewan's Sudetendeutsche: The Anti-Nazi Germans of St. Walburg," *Saskatchewan History* 33, no. 3 (autumn 1980): 90–92.
22. Everett Baker, "Visiting a Group of Sudeten Settlers," *The Western Producer*, 20 July 1939, 19.
23. Wagner, "Saskatchewan's Sudetendeutsche," 92–94.
24. Ibid., 95.
25. "I certainly didn't like to part with my Leica, but now I am glad you bought it." SAB, Everett Baker papers, R561, f. 13C, H. Haas to E. Baker, 7 February 1943. It has been suggested elsewhere that Baker bought the camera from Haas's son Gabriel, but he is not the author of the cited letter. Haas later moved to Edmonton but stayed in touch with Baker through the 1940s.
26. SAB, Everett Baker papers, R561, f. 13A, E. Baker to Canadian National Railways, 6 November 1940.
27. Smith, "Picturing," 18. The incorporation of the camera into Baker's work was an example of how Pool field men continually employed new media technology to enhance their popularity as entertainers. MacPherson, "Missionaries," 96.
28. Moose Jaw Museum and Art Gallery, Alice Allen interview, 6 March 2006.
29. Fairbairn, "Everett Baker," 39.
30. "Through the Eyes of Everett Baker," <http://www.virtual.museum.ca>.
31. Halderman interview.
32. Jim Forrest, interview by author, 21 June 2006.
33. SWP, Baker Folder 1, "A Few Thoughts and Some History on the Saskatchewan History and Folklore Society," n.d. (probably 1967–68).

34. SAB, Everett Baker papers, R561, f. 38, R. H. Simmonds to E. Baker, 3 April 1978.
35. Waiser, *Saskatchewan*, 353-57.
36. Sharon Butala, "Time, Space, and Lighting: Discovering the Saskatchewan Soul," *NeWest Review* 13, no. 6 (February 1988): 4.
37. Waiser, *Saskatchewan*, 361-73. For a personal account of the impact of these changes on the farm, see Ted Turner's interview in Robert Collins, *You Had to Be There* (Toronto: McClelland and Stewart, 1997), 199-203.
38. SAB, Everett Baker papers, R561, f. 30H, "What's in a Name?"
39. Everett Baker, "A Tour of Rebellion Battlefields," *Saskatchewan History* 3, no. 1 (winter 1950): 32. Baker served two terms on the advisory board for the journal.
40. Baker, interview.
41. Waiser, *Saskatchewan*, 346-47.
42. SAB, Everett Baker papers, R561, f. 31B.
43. Most of these pictures were taken with a new camera, a Japanese model, after his Leica was stolen in Cypress Hills Park. Smith, "Picturing," 19.
44. Baker, "A Few Thoughts."
45. See P. F. Rein, "These Changing Conditions: A Study of the Saskatchewan Royal Commission on Agriculture and Rural Life" (master's thesis, University of Regina, 1994).
46. Everett Baker, *Trails and Traces of Rupert's Land and the North-West Territories as seen from 1940-1955* (Shaunavon, SK: Everett Baker, 1955). The collection is subtitled, "No. 1 Bits of Saskatchewan in color."
47. SAB, Everett Baker papers, R561, f. 30H, "Tape-Recorded Minutes of Saskatchewan Folklore Committee."
48. SAB, Everett Baker papers, R561, f. 30H, "A Permanent Organization?"
49. SAB, Everett Baker papers, R561, f. 30B. E. Baker to B. Davies, 24 February 1958; Smith, "Picturing," 20-21.
50. SAB, Everett Baker papers, R561, f. 30C, E. Baker to A. Turner, 29 January 1959.
51. Baker, "A Few Thoughts."
52. Ibid.
53. Ibid.
54. "Rebuilding Prairie Trails," *RCMP Quarterly* 27, no. 1 (July 1961): 3-5.
55. *Leader-Post* (Regina), 12 October 1963.
56. SAB, Everett Baker papers, R563, f. 38, E. Baker to H. Robson, 20 November 1966.
57. The Eastend Educational Association formally recognized Baker, Shepherd, and Jones for their work in 1964.
58. SAB, Everett Baker papers, R563, f. 38, E. Baker to D. Tatchell, 7 March 1969.
59. SWP, Baker Folder 2, E. Baker to Minister of Citizenship and Immigration, 30 December 1970.
60. Michael Gillgannon, "In on ground floor of history," *Co-operative Consumer* 34, no. 20 (31 October 1972): 1.

APPENDIX: THE LEICA CAMERA AND KODACHROME FILM

61. A. Pasi, *Leica: Witness to a Century* (New York: W. W. Norton, 2003), 18.
62. W. D. Morgan, *The Leica Manual: A Manual for the Amateur and Professional Covering the Field of Miniature Camera Photography* (New York: Morgan and Lester, 1935), 6.
63. "Exhibition of Leica Camera Photography," *Globe & Mail*, 10 February 1936, p. 3.
64. P. Krause, "Kodachrome's Colorful History," *Modern Photography*, October 1985, 83.
65. Ibid., 63.

FURTHER READING ON THE HISTORY OF PHOTOGRAPHY

Coe, B., and P. Gates. *The Snapshot Photograph: The Rise of Popular Photography, 1888-1939*. London: Ash and Grant, 1977.

Eder, J. M. *History of Photography*. New York: Dover Publications, 1978.

Freund, G. *Photography and Society*. Boston: David R. Godine, 1980.

Keppler, V. *The Eighth Art: A Life of Color Photography*. New York: William Morrow, 1938.

Rijper, E. *Kodachrome: The American Invention of Our World 1939-1959*. New York: Delano Greenridge Editions, 2002.

ACKNOWLEDGEMENTS

Everett Baker's Saskatchewan would not have been possible without the foresight of the Saskatchewan History & Folklore Society, which provided a welcome home for the Baker slide collection a decade ago and has been actively promoting its significance and uniqueness ever since. A special thank you is owed to executive director Finn Andersen, who did everything possible to facilitate the book project, including sharing his unrivalled knowledge of the collection.

Brock Silversides generously offered to prepare an appendix about the camera and film used by Baker, and thereby added a specialist's touch to the story. Jim Miller and Marley Waiser kindly read and commented on an early draft. Their helpful feedback is gratefully acknowledged.

Kirsten Craven knocked the rough edges off my writing with her editing skills. Brian Smith and Mike McCoy of Articulate Eye delivered another stunning design. And Meaghan Craven carefully shepherded the project through the various production stages with her infectious enthusiasm.

Fifth House was interested in doing the Baker book when it was only a vague idea. Publisher Charlene Dobmeier appreciated the importance of the Baker photographs to Saskatchewan history. In fact, she could see her own family's experience and that of countless others in the pictures. That's why the Baker collection is so special today. Even though the images capture a time and place that might seem light years away, people readily identify with them thanks to Baker's skill with his camera. It's a good thing he liked to take pictures. He, most of all, rightfully deserves our gratitude.

INDEX OF PLACES PHOTOGRAPHED BY EVERETT BAKER

Admiral, 24–27
Algrove, 28
Aneroid, 29–34
Arran, 35
Batoche, 36
Battle Creek, 37
Beaver Lake, 38
Bracken, 39–41
Brightsand, 42
Cadillac, 43–45
Canuck, 46–47
Carrot River, 48–49
Chambery, 50
Claydon, 51–52
Climax, 53–60
Compass, 61
Consul, 62
Crichton, 62–63
Cut Knife, 64
Cypress Hills, 65
Debden, 66
Divide, 67–69
Dollard, 70
Dorintosh, 71
Duck Lake, 71–73
Eastend, 74–80
Ferland, 81
Fort Qu'Appelle, 82–83

Frenchman Butte, 84–86
Frontier, 87
Garden Head, 88
Glentworth, 89
Gouverneur, 90
Gravelbourg, 91
Greig Lake, 92
Hazenmore, 93–95
Hudson Bay, 96
Instow, 97
Island Lake, 98
Kenosee Lake, 11, 99–100
Killdeer, 101
Kincaid, 102
Klintonel, 103
La Ronge, 104
Lac Pelletier, 104–106
Lashburn, 107
Liberty, 108–109
Lloydminster, 110
Loon Lake, 111–13
Makwa, 9, 114
Mankota, 115–17
Maple Creek, 118–20
Matador, 121–23
McCord, 124–25
Melfort, 126–27
Meskanaw, 128

Meyronne, 129
Moose Jaw, 130–31
North Battleford, 132–33
North Fork, 134–36
Onion Lake, 136
Peck Lake, 137
Ponteix, 137–40
Prince Albert, 141–43
Ravenscrag, 144–48
Regina, 148–52
Reliance, 153–54
Robsart, 155
Rosefield, 156
Saskatchewan Landing, 157
Saskatoon, 158–60
Shaunavon, 161–73
South Fork, 174–75
Swift Current, 176
Unity, 177
Val Marie, 5, 178–80
Veregin, 181
Wakaw, 182–83
Waskesiu, 184
Waterhen, 185
Watrous, 186–87
Wolseley, 188
Wood Mountain, 189
Yorkton, 190–91

ABOUT THE AUTHOR

Bill Waiser has been a member of the history department at the University of Saskatchewan since 1984. Prior to his Saskatchewan appointment, Bill served as Yukon historian for Parks Canada's Prairie and Northern Regional Office (1983–1984).

A specialist in western and northern Canadian history, Bill is an instructor at both the undergraduate and graduate level. In May 2002, he was awarded the College of Arts and Science Teaching Excellence Award for the Humanities and Fine Arts. Bill has also served as a member of the Canadian Historical Association Council (1997–2000); chaired the advisory board of the Canadian Historical Review (2000–2003); and been a member of the board of directors of Canada's National History Society (2001–2004), the publisher of *The Beaver* magazine.

Bill is the author, co-author, or co-editor of nine books, including *Park Prisoners: The Untold Story of Western Canada's National Parks* and (with Blair Stonechild) *Loyal Till Death: Indians and the North-West Rebellion*, which was a 1997 finalist for the Governor General's Literary Award for Nonfiction. His book *All Hell Can't Stop Us: The On-To-Ottawa Trek and Regina Riot* won the 2003 nonfiction prize at the Saskatchewan Book Awards. Bill's most recent book, *Saskatchewan: A New History*, was presented to Her Majesty Queen Elizabeth II at a University of Saskatchewan ceremony in May 2005 and given to all of the schools in the province as a centennial gift. *Saskatchewan: A New History* was also named the best book in prairie history in 2005 (Clio Prize) by the Canadian Historical Association.

Between 1998 and 2002, Bill served as host of *Looking Back*, a weekly Saskatchewan history column on the early evening news broadcast of CBC Saskatchewan. The series won an honourable mention at the Columbus International Film and Video Festival in 2004. In 2006, the lieutenant-governor of Saskatchewan presented Bill with the Saskatchewan Order of Merit, the province's highest honour. He was named recipient of the University of Saskatchewan Alumni Honour Award that same year.

Bill is a recreational runner, who also likes to hike, garden, and canoe.

ABOUT FIFTH HOUSE

Fifth House Publishers, a Fitzhenry & Whiteside company, is a proudly western-Canadian press. Our publishing specialty is non-fiction as we believe that every community must possess a positive understanding of its worth and place if it is to remain vital and progressive. Fifth House is committed to "bringing the West to the rest" by publishing approximately twenty books a year about the land and people who make this region unique. Our books are selected for their quality and contribution to the understanding of western-Canadian (and Canadian) history, culture, and environment.

Look for the following Fifth House titles at your local bookstore:

The Face Pullers: Photographing Native Canadians, 1871–1939, Brock V. Silversides

Looking Back: True Tales from Saskatchewan's Past, Paul Dederick and Bill Waiser

Looking West: Photographing the Canadian Prairies, 1858–1957, Brock V. Silversides

Prairie Sentinel: The Story of the Canadian Grain Elevator, Brock V. Silversides

Saskatchewan: A New History, Bill Waiser

Shooting Cowboys: Photographing Canadian Cowboy Culture, 1875–1965, Brock V. Silversides

Tommy Douglas: The Road to Jerusalem, Thomas H. McLeod and Ian McLeod

What's in a Name? The Story Behind Saskatchewan Place Names, E. T. Russell

Where the River Runs: Stories of the Saskatchewan and the People Drawn to Its Shores, Victor Carl Friesen